ISBN 978-0-243-10171-9
PIBN 10763772

1 MONTH OF
FREE
READING

at

www.ForgottenBooks.com

By purchasing this book you are
eligible for one month membership to
ForgottenBooks.com, giving you
unlimited access to our entire
collection of over 700,000 titles via
our web site and mobile apps.

To claim your free month visit:

www.forgottenbooks.com/free763772

English
Français
Deutsche
Italiano
Español
Português

www.forgottenbooks.com

Mythology Photography **Fiction**
Fishing Christianity **Art** Cooking
Essays Buddhism Freemasonry
Medicine **Biology** Music **Ancient**
Egypt Evolution Carpentry Physics
Dance Geology **Mathematics** Fitness
Shakespeare **Folklore** Yoga Marketing
Confidence Immortality Biographies
Poetry **Psychology** Witchcraft
Electronics Chemistry History **Law**
Accounting **Philosophy** Anthropology
Alchemy Drama Quantum Mechanics
Atheism Sexual Health **Ancient History**
Entrepreneurship Languages Sport
Paleontology Needlework Islam
Metaphysics Investment Archaeology
Parenting Statistics Criminology
Motivational

ANNUAL REPORT

OF THE

TOWN OF HAVERHILL

YEAR ENDING

FEBRUARY 15

1 9 1 4

ANNUAL REPORT

OF THE

TOWN OFFICERS

OF THE

TOWN OF

HAVERHILL

NEW HAMPSHIRE

FOR THE YEAR ENDING

FEBRUARY 15, 1914

WOODSVILLE, N. H.
NEWS PRINT
1914.

OFFICERS OF THE TOWN OF HAVERHILL

MODERATOR
William F. Whitcher,   Woodsville

TOWN CLERK
Albert F. Kimball,   North Haverhill

SELECTMEN
Charles J. Pike (Resigned July 21, 1913),   Haverhill
Henry W. Keyes (Appointed Aug. 26, 1913), North Haverhill
William J. Clough,   North Haverhill
Dexter L. Hawkins,   Woodsville

TREASURER
Louis M. Kimball,   North Haverhill

SCHOOL BOARD
E. Blank,   Pike
Jesse R. Squires,   Haverhill
William E. Lawrence,   North Haverhill

BOARD OF HEALTH
E. B. Willoughby,   North Haverhill
C. H. Johnson,   Woodsville
P. W. Allen,   East Haverhill

AUDITORS
William F. Whitcher,   Woodsville
Norman J. Page,   Woodsville

TAX COLLECTOR
Charles S. Newell,   Woodsville

HIGHWAY AGENTS
Thomas Morris,   Haverhill
Manson F. Young,   Pike
Irving W. Thayer,   North Haverhill

SUPERVISORS

Walter Burbeck,	Woodsville
Willard W. Coburn,	North Haverhill
Pardon W. Allen,	East Haverhill

LIBRARY TRUSTEES

Fred P. Dearth,	Woodsville
Jesse R. Squires,	Haverhill
Moses A. Meader,	North Haverhill

FENCE VIEWERS

George F. Kimball,	North Haverhill
George C. Jeffers,	East Haverhill
M. S. Williams,	Haverhill

SEALERS OF WEIGHTS AND MEASURES

E. M. Morrison,	Haverhill
J. F. Leonard,	Woodsville

SUPERVISORS OF WOOD AND LUMBER

Joseph Willis,	Woodsville
W. W. Coburn,	North Haverhill
W. F. True,	East Haverhill
Jesse R. Squires,	Haverhill
P. W. Allen,	East Haverhill
C. A. Wood,	Haverhill

CEMETERY COMMISSIONERS

E. B. Willoughby,	North Haverhill
P. W. Kimball,	Haverhill
J. M. Jeffers,	East Haverhill
L. E. Glazier,	Center Haverhill
E. Bertram Pike,	Pike

SPECIAL POLICE

A. E. Davis,	Woodsville
C. S. Newell,	Woodsville
J. C. Gallagher,	Woodsville
Percy Deming,	North Haverhill
W. A. Davis,	Pike
Frank L. Keyes,	Haverhill

WARRANT FOR ANNUAL TOWN MEETING, 1914.

[L.S.] THE STATE OF NEW HAMPSHIRE

To the Inhabitants of the Town of Haverhill qualified to vote in town affairs:

You are hereby notified to meet at the Town Hall in said town on the second Tuesday of March next at ten of the clock in the forenoon to act upon the following matters:

ARTICLE 1. To choose a town clerk.

ART. 2. To choose three selectmen.

ART. 3. To choose a town treasurer.

ART. 4. To choose one or more highway agents.

ART. 5. To choose one or more auditors.

ART. 6. To choose one library trustee for the term of three years.

ART. 7. To choose one member of the board of cemetery commissioners for the term of five years.

ART. 8. To see if the town will vote to elect tax assessors; and if so, to determine the number of assessors and to choose the same.

ART. 9. To choose all other necessary town officers.

ART. 10. To hear the reports of the selectmen, treasurer, cemetery commissioners, and other town officers heretofore chosen, and to pass any vote relating thereto.

ART. 11. To see if the town will vote to authorize the selectmen to borrow on the credit of the town such sums of money as may be needed to defray town expenses until the taxes shall be collected, and to issue the notes of the town for all sums so borrowed.

ART. 12. To see if the town will vote to adopt the provisions of chapter 124 of the Public Statutes, relating to dealers in old metals.

ART. 13. To raise and appropriate such sums of money as may be necessary for the maintenance of the poor.

ART. 14. To raise and appropriate such sum of money as may be necessary to retire three thousand dollars of town bonds and to pay interest on bonds outstanding.

ART. 15. To raise and appropriate such sum of money as may be necessary for laying out, building and repairing highways, and for building and repairing bridges.

ART. 16. To see what action the town will take in regard to securing state aid for highways in this town under the provisions of an act approved February 24, 1903, entitled "An act to provide for state aid and for the expenditures of other public moneys in the permanent improvement of main highways throughout the state," and acts in amendment thereof; to raise and appropriate such sum of money as may be deemed advisable for expenditure under the provisions of said act and amendments; and to pass any other vote relating thereto.

ART. 17. To determine what sum of money the town will raise and appropriate for the town libraries.

ART. 18. To determine what sum of money the town will raise and appropriate for the North Haverhill Public Library in addition to that required by law.

ART. 19. To determine what sum of money the town will raise and appropriate for Decoration Day.

ART. 20. To see if the town will vote to raise and appropriate a sum of money not exceeding three hundred dollars for a free hospital bed at Cottage Hospital in Haverhill, for the period of one year; and if so, to elect an agent or agents to expend the sum so raised; and to pass any other vote relating thereto.

ART. 21. To see what action the town will take in regard to repairing and improving the Town Hall; to raise and appropriate money for that purpose; and to pass any other vote relating thereto.

ART. 22.   To see if the town will vote to light the highway running Easterly and Southerly from the Easterly end of the Haverhill Bridge to the River Road, so called; to raise and appropriate money for that purpose; and to pass any other vote relating thereto.

ART. 23.   To raise and appropriate such sums of money as may be necessary for other town charges.

Given under our hands and seal this twenty-first day of February, A. D. 1914.

> HENRY W. KEYES,
> WILLIAM J. CLOUGH,
> DEXTER L. HAWKINS,
> *Selectmen of Haverhill.*

A true copy of warrant.   Attest:

> HENRY W. KEYES,
> WILLIAM J. CLOUGH,
> DEXTER L. HAWKINS,
> *Selectmen of Haverhill.*

TREASURER'S REPORT

To the Taxpayers of the Town of Haverhill, N. H.:

Herewith is my report as Town Treasurer for the year ending February 15, 1914:

RECEIPTS

Balance in Treasury February 15, 1913,		$8,391.67
Received taxes redeemed,		411.28
Received rent of leased lands,		106.94
Grafton County Poor,		643.27
Dependent soldiers,		134.00
State treasurer,		
highway,		4,280.29
forestry bills,		23.66
railroad tax,		2,942.42
savings bank tax,		3,217.63
literary fund,		498.18
school fund,		2,507.18
Dog licenses,		525.20
Liquor and other licenses,		367.45
Haverhill Police Court,		322.38
Sale of gravel,		139.90
Sale of bridge,		56.23
Rent of town hall,		58.76
Sheep killed,		13.00
Received refund on permanent highway overdraft,		1,361.27
Received Charles S. Newell, collector,		47,391.84
Received income Southard Fund,		
Laconia town bonds,		160.00
Savings bank book,	$32.30	
Less amount redeposited,	28.30	
		4.00

Received Income A. M. Lyman fund,	$4.05
Franklin Crouch fund,	17.97
John W. Jackson fund,	3.55
T. B. Jackson fund,	3.55
Emily K. Garland, fund,	2.68
Solon H. Baker fund,	1.74
Hosea S. Baker fund,	1.79
Charles G. Smith fund,	7.07
Ida M. Hunt fund,	10.75
R. E. Webster fund,	3.53
Burns Pike fund,	.88
E. B. Pike fund,	17.77
Relatives E. B. Pike,	17.77
Harriet Platt,	5.87
Received refund permanent highway maintenance,	
W. J. Clough,	41.24

$73,696.76

DISBURSEMENTS

Paid selectmen's orders for:	
Highways,	$3,565.96
Police,	477.14
Town expense,	2,179.91
County poor,	652.77
Town schools,	11,303.76
Woodsville schools,	9,070.49
Woodsville precinct (fire district),	7,548.85
Water troughs,	81.00
Quarantine,	413.91
Miscellaneous,	18,710.45
Haverhill precinct,	600.00
Town libraries,	300.00
Dog license fund,	74.00
Permanent highway,	6,000.00
Permanent highway maintenance,	1,194.39
Special appropriation, for highway,	2,028.37

$64,201.00

Paid State tax, $4,848.00
Cash on hand February 16, 1914,   4,647.76
                                         _____

                                         $73,696.76

Town bonds due December 1, 1913, number 43, 44, 45, totaling $3,000; also interest on bonded debt amounting to $600 included in miscellaneous orders.

There are no outstanding orders.

Respectfully submitted,

LOUIS M. KIMBALL,
Town Treasurer.

HAVERHILL, N. H., February 16, 1914.

REPORT OF THE SELECTMEN

To the Citizens and Taxpayers of Haverhill:

The selectmen submit herewith their report for the year ending February 15, 1914.

It is the desire of the selectmen to present such a report as will give the taxpayers a clear understanding of their town affairs, and they think they have done so in the information given on the following pages. Many taxpayers do not wish to spend the time (which is to be regretted) to look through the details of a town report, and your selectmen, therefore, would briefly call your attention to a few facts and statements.

The valuation of the town the past year shows a slight decrease, noticeably—the item of money at interest. The town is owing no notes, and has no outstanding orders. Payment has been made of $3,000 of town bonds, leaving the amount of bonds outstanding $12,000.

It is gratifying to note that there were no paupers chargeable to the town during the past year and that the County Poor and Quarantine accounts both show a decrease from last year.

As to highways: for ordinary repairs there was about the usual amount expended. At the last March meeting the town voted a special appropriation of $2,000 and this money was expended on two roads; the road running easterly from North Haverhill to Pike and the Oliverian Brook road. The state highway (or Trunk Line, so called), follows the Connecticut River from the Piermont town line to Cottage Hospital and thence easterly to the Bath town line. From Piermont line to said hospital the road was completed last year. Money was raised at the last town meeting to complete this highway from the hospital to the Bath line, but the state highway department was unable to finish its work. It should be remembered, however, that there is sufficient money provided to complete this highway. Acting upon a vote of the town as to repairing the old Haverhill-Newbury bridge or building a new bridge, your board, acting with the selectmen of Newbury, Vt., decided it was for the interest of the town to build a new bridge. No appropriation was made for this bridge, but a new first-class steel bridge, with concrete flooring, has been built and the pier and abutments strongly re-enforced with cement and iron. The total cost of the bridge was a little over $20,000 making the cost to the town of Haverhill about $10,000, all of which has been paid.

The net debt of the town is now $8,464.37 which is an increase of $2,394.86 over last year. This increase was brought about by paying for the Haverhill-Newbury bridge. Had the town raised money to pay for this bridge it would today be practically out of debt.

In closing this report, your selectmen wish to record the great loss which the town has sustained in the removal by death of Charles J. Pike, who last March was your choice for first selectman. His service for a period of nearly seventeen years was marked by faithful and devoted efficiency, for which the members of the present board, each of whom had served with him as a colleague, wish to express unqualified appreciation. By his death the town loses one of its most useful and honored citizens.

Following is the report in detail:

HIGHWAYS

Appropriation:

    Proportion of $5,000 raised at March meeting, $2,601.15

Orders drawn:

Thomas Morris,	$56.66
H. W. Dexter,	10.15
Manson F. Young,	94.00
Thomas Morris,	141.64
J. M. Nutter, hanging lantern on washout,	3.00
Thomas Morris,	198.07
Manson F. Young,	75.93
Irving W. Thayer,	61.37
Manson F. Young,	384.50
Irving W. Thayer,	29.06
Thomas Morris,	326.32
Thomas Morris,	122.26
Irving W. Thayer,	35.83
F. L. Blake, road machine blades,	8.50
New England Road Machine Co., road machine blades,	8.50
Irving W. Thayer,	468.83
Thomas Morris,	69.44
Manson F. Young,	94.00
Irving W. Thayer,	126.65
Manson F. Young,	29.00
Thomas Morris,	69.30
Manson F. Young,	39.71
Thomas Morris,	127.10
Manson F. Young,	104.91
Thomas Morris,	48.52
Irving W. Thayer,	47.59
E. W. Shaw,	36.00
E. Bertram Pike,	500.00
Canton Bridge Co., one culvert,	21.17
Manson F. Young,	30.60

Orders drawn:

Thomas Morris,	$45.11
Joseph Henderson,	3.40
Irving W. Thayer,	15.25
Thomas Morris,.	49.00
Manson F. Young,	70.00
Irving W. Thayer,	10.44
Kimball Brothers, supplies for road agents,	4.15

$3,565.96

Included in the above are orders drawn to the road agents amounting to $2,981.24, which they report expended as follows:

H. W. DEXTER,—$10.15

1912.

March—H. W. Dexter, 3 days; team, 1 day,	$8.00
G. Cutting, 1 day,	1.75
P. Dargie, 8 loads grade,	.40

$10.15

THOMAS MORRIS,—$1,253.42

1913.

March—Thomas Morris, 6 days,	$12.00
Man, 7 days; team, 7 days,	28.00
Man, 3 days,	5.25
W. H. Morris, man, 1 day; team, 1 day,	4.00
Man, 1 day,	1.75
Pike Mfg. Co., man 13½ hours; team, 13½ hours,	5.40
Man, 1½ hours,	.26

$56.66

April—Thomas Morris, 6½ days,	$13.00
1 shovel,	.60
Nails and spikes,	.40

April— Man and team, 14 days, $56.00
         Man, 13 days,   22.75
         W. H. Morris, man, 7½ days;
         team, 7½ days,   30.00
         Man, 1½ days,   2.63
         Elmer Spencer, repairing road
         machine,   3.50
         Pike Mfg. Co., man, 2 days;
         team, 2 days,   8.00
         39 lbs. iron at 4¢ lb.,   1.56
         Willis Kelley, 36 loads grade
         at 5¢,   1.80
         George Wells, 5 loads grade
         at 5¢,   .25
         C. J. Pike, 10 loads grade at
         5¢,   .50
         Mrs. St. Clair, 7 loads grade
         at 5¢,   .35
         F. J. Winn, 6 loads grade at
         5¢,   .30
                                  ———— $141.64

May—Thomas Morris, 17 days, $34.00
         Spikes,   .50
         Repairs on machine,   .50
         Man on machine, 10½ days,   21.00
         Man, 1½ days,   2.63
         Man and team, 3½ days,   14.00
         Man and three horses, 10½
         days,   52.50
         W. H. Morris, man and team,
         11 days,   44.00
         Man, 5½ days,   9.63
         170 feet timber at $20 M.,   3.40
         W. E. Marston, labor on
         bridge,   2.00
         Pike Mfg. Co., man and
         team, 12½ hours,   4.40
         Man, 1 hour,   .18

May— C. J. Pike, 7 loads grade at
5¢, $0.35

E. M. Clark, 449 feet plank
at $20 M.,   8.98

                                             $198.07

June—Thomas Morris, 22½ days, $45.00

Man and 3 horses, 8 days,   40.00

Man and 2 horses, 14 days,   56.00

Man on machine, 15 days,   30.00

Spikes and repairs,   1.00

W. H. Morris, man and team,
21½ days,   86.00

Man, 10½ days,   18.37

L. M. Wheeler, self and team,
7 days,   28.00

Willis Kelley, 54 loads grade
at 5¢,   2.70

Pike Mfg. Co., repairing
machine,   9.50

F. L. Blake, 1 machine blade,   8.00

Harry Merchant, 1 day,   1.75

                                             $326.32

July—Thomas Morris, 5½ days, $11.00

Man and team, 4½ days,   18.00

W. H. Morris, man and team,
3¼ days,   13.00

Man, 3 days,   5.25

James Ralston, self and team,
17 hours,   6.80

Man, 2½ hours,   .50

F. L. Keyes, blasting,   1.00

Pike Mfg. Co., labor and
supplies,   -   14.08

Fayette Bacon, 2,196 feet
plank at $18 M.,   39.52

E. M. Clark, 618 feet plank at
$20 M.,   12.36

July— George Wells, 15 loads grade
       at 5¢, $0.75

                                                $122.26

Aug.—Thomas Morris, 9½ days, $19.00
       Man and team, 8 days,   32.00
       72 feet timber at $18 M.,   1.29
       W. H. Morris, man and team,
         3½ days,   14.00
       Pike Mfg. Co., 10 sticks
         dynamite at 15¢,   1.50
       12 exploding caps,   .75
       Mrs. St. Clair, 7 loads grade
        at 5¢,   .35
       George Wells, 11 loads grade
        at 5¢,   .55

                                                  $69.44

Sept.—Thomas Morris, 7 days, $14.00
       Man and team, 10 days,   40.00
       Man, 4 days,   7.00
       W. H. Morris, man and
        team, 1½ days,   6.00
       J. Henderson, 7 loads grade
        at 5¢,   .35
       George Wells, 14 loads grade
        at 5¢,   .70
       Willis Kelley, 25 loads grade
        at 5¢,   1.25

                                                  $69.30

Oct.—Thomas Morris, 16 days, $32.00
       Man and team, 11 days,   44.00
       35 lbs. spikes at 3½¢,   1.23
       1 bag cement,   .65
       16 cedar posts at 14¢,   2.24
       W. H. Morris, man and
        team, 4¾ days,   19.00
       180 feet bridge timber at
        $20 M.,   3.60

Oct.— George B. Silver, labor man
　　　　and team,　　　　　　　　　　$19.58
　　　Mrs. St. Clair, 17 loads grade
　　　　at 5¢,　　　　　　　　　　　　.85
　　　Willis Kelley, 35 loads grade
　　　　at $5¢,　　　　　　　　　　　1.75
　　　H. S. Bailey, 14 loads grade
　　　　at 5¢,　　　　　　　　　　　　.70
　　　George Wells, 30 loads grade
　　　　at 5¢,　　　　　　　　　　　1.50
　　　　　　　　　　　　　　　　　　　　　　　$127.10

Nov.—Thomas Morris, 3 days,　　　　$6.00
　　　Man and team, 3 days,　　　　12.00
　　　F. Sleeper, 776 feet plank
　　　　at $20 M.,　　　　　　　　15.52
　　　W. H. Ingalls and man, 2½
　　　　days,　　　　　　　　　　15.00
　　　　　　　　　　　　　　　　　　　　　　　$48.52

Dec.—Thomas Morris, 5 days,　　　$10.00
　　　Man and team, 3 days,　　　12.00
　　　Repairing roller,　　　　　　2.00
　　　W. H. Morris, man and team,
　　　　2 days,　　　　　　　　　　8.00
　　　A. K. Merrill, 1 day,　　　　2.00
　　　Spikes,　　　　　　　　　　　.20
　　　F. S. Sleeper, 3 pieces 8 x 8
　　　　x 16 at $22 M.,　　　　　　.63
　　　264 feet plank at $20 M.,　　5.28
　　　　　　　　　　　　　　　　　　　　　　　$45.11
　　1914.
Jan.—Thomas Morris, 3 days,　　　　$6.00
　　　Man and team, 5½ days,　　　22.00
　　　W. H. Morris, man and team,
　　　　5¼ days,　　　　　　　　　21.00
　　　　　　　　　　　　　　　　　　　　　　　$49.00

　　　　　　　　　　　　　　　　　　　　　　$1,253.42

MANSON F. YOUNG,—$922.65

1913.

March—M. F. Young, 5 days, 8 hours,	$11.60	
Man, 4 days, 9 hours, with team,	19.60	
Fred Aldrich, man and team, 5 hours,	2.00	
Fred Clark, man and team, 2½ hours,	1.00	
Sam Elliott, 5 days,	8.75	
E. S. Everett, 2 days,	3.50	
		$46.45
April—M. F. Young, 6 days,	$12.00	
Man and team, 7 days, 1 hour,	28.40	
E. C. French, 1 day, 8 hours,	3.05	
Sam Elliott, 1 day, 8 hours,	3.05	
Charles A. Gale, 7 hours,	1.05	
		$47.55
May—Manson F. Young, 6 days,	$12.00	
Man and team, 8 days,	32.00	
Pick and handle,	.60	
Man, 2 days, 9 hours,	3.22	
Charles Halfird, 1 day,	1.75	
George Cutting, 6½ days,	11.37	
J. N. Brown, 2½ days,	6.25	
J. N. Brown, team, 2½ days,	5.00	
Machine Work:		
Frank Shallow, man and team, ½ day,	2.00	
Frank Aldrich, ½ day,	.87	
Fred Aldrich, ½ day,	.87	
		$75.93
June—M. F. Young, 24 days,	$48.00	
M. F. Young, man and team, 49½ days,	198.00	
J. N. Brown, 23 days,	57.50	

June— J. N. Brown, team, 23 days, $46.00

      Charles Halfird, 19 days,   33.25

      Nat. Clark, 1 day,   1.75

                        $384.50

Aug.—Manson F. Young, 13½ days, $27.00

      Manson F. Young, man and

        team, 16¾ days,   67.00

                        $94.00

Sept.—Manson F. Young, 4 days;

        team, 4 days, $24.00

      Pike Mfg. Co., repairing road

        machine,   5.00

                        $29.00

Oct.—Manson F. Young, 4½ days, $9.00

      Man and team, 4 days,   16.00

      W. B. Titus, 7 hours,   1.35

      W. B. Titus, 576 feet 3-inch

        plank,   10.36

      W. B. Titus, 200 feet 6 x 6,   3.00

                        $39.71

Nov.—Manson F. Young, 11½ days, $23.00

      Man and team, 7 days,   28.00

      Westley White, 1½ days,   2.62

      Fayette Bacon, bridge plank,   50.69

      W. B. Titus, 4 stringers,   .60

                        $104.91

Dec.—Manson F. Young, 1 day; team,

        1 day, $4.00

      E. G. Hobbs, man and team,

        2 days,   8.00

      S. L. Clifford, 304 feet bridge

        plank,   6.08

      Man and team, ½ day,   2.00

      Elward Everett, 3½ days,   6.12

      E. Boardman, housing roller,   2.00

      F. R. Dean, 16 loads grading,   .80

Dec.— Damon Gannett, 17 loads
grading, $0.85
Charles Perkins, 15 loads
grading,   .75
                                         $30.60

1914.

Jan.—Manson F. Young, 1¼ days;
team, 1¼ days, $5.00
Nat. Clark, 17 hours,   2.98
J. A. Howard, 13 hours; team,
13 hours,   5.20
H. W. Dexter, 20 hours; team,
20 hours,   8.00
E. M. Clark, 1,835 feet plank
and stringers,   40.37
Wilbur Pike, repairing road
machine,   4.95
Sam Elliott, man, 2 days,   3.50
                                           $70.00

                                         $922.65

IRVING W. THAYER,—$795.02

1913.

March—Irving Thayer, 13 hours;
team, 13 hours, $5.85
Ray Kimball, 10 hours; team,
4 hours,   2.60
Man, 4 hours,   .80
April—Irving Thayer, 18 hours;
team, 18 hours,   8.10
Ray Kimball, 19 hours; team,
17 hours,   7.97
Man, 17 hours,   3.35
Mike Keith, 41 hours; team,
28 hours,   13.95
Man, 8 hours,   1.60

April— Mike Keith, boy and team,
     5 hours, $2.65
     Ralph Rogers, 6 hours,   1.20
May—Irving Thayer, 4 hours; team,
     4 hours,   1.80
     J. French, 18 hours; team, 18
     hours,   .00
     Man, 18 hours,   8.50

                                         $61.37
June—Irving Thayer, 57 hours; team,
     24 hours, $16.66
     Silas Hurlburt 36 hours,   7.00
     Roy Cotton, 13½ hours,   1.89
     Ernest W. Nelson, 10½ hours;
     team, 6 hours,   3.51

                                       $29.06
July—Irving Thayer, 1 day; team, 1
     day, $4.00
     Frank Blake, 1 day,   1.75
     D. S. Merrill,   21.40
     Charles Chase, 6 horses, 6
     hours,   5.34
     Charles Chase, man, 6 hours,   2.34
     Charles Chase, 20 loads
     grade,   1.00

                                     $35.83
Aug.—Irving Thayer, 25 days; team,
     25 days, $100.00
     Arthur Kimball, 24 days;
     team, 24 days,   96.00
     Ray Kimball, 24 days; team,
     24 days,   96.00
     Frank Blake, 25 days,   62.50
     Arthur Kimball's man, 10
     days,   20.00
     E. J. Nelson, 24½ days,   49.00
     Ray Kimball's man, 1½ days,   3.00
     K. Robertson, 4 days,   8.00

Aug.— William Coats, 3 days; team,
    3 days, $2.00
Charles Chase, 2 day; team,
    1 day,   4.00
R. W. Rogers, 2 days, 5 hours;
    team, 2 days,
    5 hours,   10.23
W. M. Thayer, 1 day,   1.75
W. M. Thayer, 8 hours, with
    team,   3.20
Express on road machine
    blade,   1.15
Bolts and fixtures for road
    machine,   2.00
                                  $468.83

Sept.—Irving Thayer, 6½ days; team,
    6½ days, $26.00
Frank Blake, 6½ days,   16.25
Ray Kimball, 6 days; team,
    6 days,   24.00
Arthur Kimball, team, 6
    days,   12.00
Ernest Nelson, 3 days; team,
    3 days,   12.00
Harley Kimball, ½ day,   1.00
Herbert Foster, 1 day,   2.00
E. J. Nelson, 6 days,   12.00
Charles Chase, 18 loads
    grade,   .90
Fayette Bacon, 1,128 feet
    plank,   20.50
                                  $126.65

Nov.—Irving Thayer, ½ day; team,
    ½ day, $2.00
A. C. Clough, 4¼ days; team,
    4¼ days,   17.00
E. B. Mann & Co., dynamite,
    fuse and caps,   1.08

Nov.— W. H. Ingalls, man and team, $24.66
      W. H. Ingalls, grade,   2.85

                                                                                     $47.59

Dec.—Arthur Kimball, 1½ days; team,
      1½ days, $6.00
      Ray Kimball, 1½ days; team,
      1½ days,   6.00
      George Gale, housing roller,   3.00
      Sharpening iron bars,   .25

                                                                                       $15.25

1914.

Jan.—Irving Thayer, ½ day; team, ½
      day, $2.00
      Irving Thayer, ¼ day; team,
      ¼ day,   1.00
      Charles Chase, 2 hours,   .44
      Arthur Kimball, 1 day; team,
      ½ day,   .00
      Man, 1 day; team, 1 day,   3.00

                                                                                      $10.44

                                                                                       $795.02

Special Highway Appropriation

Raised at March meeting, $2,000.00
Orders drawn:
  J. M. Getchell, 418 feet pine for Cold
    Spring Brook bridge, $12.54
  Thomas Morris, work on Brook
    Road,   277.20
  E. W. Shaw, work on Cold Spring
    Brook bridge,   334.69
  Rhett R. Scruggs, railing for Cold
    Spring Brook bridge,   20.30
  W. J. Clough, agent, work on Depot
    Street, North Haverhill,   1,320.54

Orders drawn:

Guy L. Southard, iron and work on
Cold Spring Brook bridge, $16.30

The United Construction Co., steel
for Cold Spring Brook bridge,   46.80

                 ———— $2,028.37

Included in the above are orders drawn to W. J. Clough and Thomas Morris, agents, which they report expended as follows:

W. J. CLOUGH,—$1,320.54

Milo G. Farnham, team, 24 days, 6 hours,	$98.66
Charles Burt, team 20 days, 7 hours,	83.11
Louis Carter, 20 days, 4 hours; team, 23 days, 5 hours,	135.01
Ed. Blumley, team, 23 days, 1 hour,	92.44
D. E. Reed, 22 days, 5 hours; team, 22 days, 5 hours;	134.88
Frank Dean, 12 days, 5 hours, team, 12 days, 5 hours,	75.33
Harry Patridge, 22 days,	49.50
Merlin Noyes, 24 days, 6 hours,	36.99
Charley Rines, 18 days, 5 hours,	37.11
Fred Palmer, 11 days, 1 hour,	22.22
G. Coats, 23 days, 4 hours,	46.89
Frank Clough, 23 days, 4 hours,	46.89
Percy Deming, 26 days,	58.50
Frank Hurlburt, 9 days,	18.00
H. Page, 10 days, 6 hours,	21.33
Frank Lynaugh, 15 days, 6 hours,	31.33
Earl Dutton,	18.48
Frank Monaco, 18 days, 5 hours,	37.11
Harvey Moses, 14 days, 5 hours,	29.11
R. French, 15 days, 6 hours,	31.33
James Sawyer, 12 days, 1 hour,	24.22
Arthur Coats, 11 days,	22.00
Will Coats, 12 days,	24.00

Merlin Noyes, painting sign boards,	$1.75
E. B. Scott, 3 pick handles,	.75
Percy Deming, pick handle, etc.,	1.38
G. L. Southard, blacksmithing,	21.80
M. H. Bailey, cement,	3.00
F. L. Blake, culvert,	22.94
W. J. Clough, 5 days,	15.00
Frank Dean, 1,023 loads grade,	51.15
E. B. Mann & Co., tile pipe,	16.96
Harry Patridge; team, 1½ days,	6.00
M. G. Farnham; team ½ day,	2.00
Percy Deming; 1½ days,	3.37
	————
	$1,320.54

THOMAS MORRIS,—$277.20

Thomas Morris, 14 days,	$28.00
Man and team 16 days,	64.00
Man, leveling, 14 days,	28.00
3 shovels,	1.80
W. H. Morris, man and team, 16 days,	64.00
L. M. Wheeler, 13 days,	22.75
Ben White, 2 days,	3.50
James Raymond, 5 days,	8.75
Harry Hadlock, 2 days,	3.50
Milo Merchant, 5 days,	8.75
John Stone, 1 day,	1.75
E. B. Martin, 4 days,	7.00
Fred Eastman, 2 days,	3.50
Pike Mfg. Co., dynamite and supplies,	10.00
F. L. Keyes, auger,	1.20
Willis Kelley, 414 loads grade at 5¢,	20.70
	————
	$277.20

Permanent Highway

State contribution,	$6,000.00	
Town contribution,	2,000.00	
Total fund,		$8,000.00
State disbursements,	$210.17	
Town disbursements,	4,638.73	
Total expenditures,		$4,848.90
		$3,151.10
Balance in state treasury,	$2,363.01	
Balance in town treasury,	788.09	
Total unexpended balance,		$3,151.10

Orders drawn:

W. J. Clough, agent,	$2,000.00	
W. J. Clough, agent,	2,000.00	
W. J. Clough, agent,	2,000.00	
		$6,000.00
Expended by town,	$4,638.73	
Check from W. J. Clough, agent,	1,361.27	
		$6,000.00

Permanent Highway—Maintenance

Total maintenance fund,		$1,555.70
State disbursements,	$19.17	
Town disbursements,	1,194.39	
		1,213.56
		$342.14
Refund of overdraft, W. J. Clough, agent,		41.24
Unexpended balance,		$383.38

Balance in town treasury,	$179.10	
Balance in state treasury,	204.28	
		$383.38

Orders drawn:

W. J. Clough, agent,	$222.83	
W. J. Clough, agent,	69.60	
J. P. Greenwood,	22.00	
Ed. Blumley,	25.00	
Ed. Shaw,	41.24	
W. H. Ingalls,	6.00	
W. J. Clough, agent,	778.19	
W. J. Clough, agent,	29.53	
		$1,194.39

POLICE.

(No appropriation is made.)

J. C. Gallagher, police services for February,	$5.00
J. G. Shepard, 1 day's service as special police,	2.00
Pike Mfg. Co., wood for Pike lobby,	1.78
Oscar E. Hall, housing tramps,	10.50
J. C. Gallagher, police services,	8.75
C. S. Newell, police services,	4.25
J. C. Gallagher, police services,	15.00
Woodsville Steam Laundry, washing bedding Woodsville lobby,	3.00
A. E. Davis, police officer fees,	21.10
D. D. Dow, police justice fees,	17.50

A. F. Mulliken & Son, 4 Yale padlocks
for lobby, $5.60
Fred J. Stevens, services as special
police, 3.00
C. S. Newell, police services, 3.75
P. W. Allen, police services, 6.00
J. C. Gallagher, police services 3
months, 15.00
Ray Kimball, care of lobby 4 months, 6.66
C. S. Newell, police services, 7.50
A. E. Davis, police services, 240.00
W. A. Davis, police services and housing
tramps, 9.75
Dexter D. Dow, police court records 5
years, 91.00
                                     ———— $477.14
Received from Haverhill Police Court, 322.38

      Net expense, $154.76

Town Expense

Appropriation, $1,500.00
Orders drawn:
    W. F. Whitcher, printing reports, $109.90
    R. U. Smith, services as assessor,
        1912, 5.20
    Bradford Electric Lighting Co.,
        lighting hall, bridge and clerk's
        office, 12.00

Orders drawn:

W. F. Whitcher, services as auditor, $10.00

W. J. Randolph, real estate transfers,   8.16

D. L. Hawkins, postage on town reports,   7.00

F. P. Dearth, renewal town treasurer's bond,   15.00

E. C. Eastman, town order book,   5.50

Bradford Electric Lighting Co., lighting,   6.00

W. J. Clough, on account services selectman,   50.00

Walter Burbeck, service as supervisor,   17.50

E. B. Mann & Co., inventory books and supplies,   5.20

Bradford Electric Lighting Co., lighting,   6.00

The Woodsville News, printing tax bills, etc.,   8.25

Bradford Electric Lighting Co., lighting,   6.00

Alberta B. Wright, work on taxes,   39.00

Bradford Electric Lighting Co., excess on lights to July 1,   7.30

C. J. Pike, services and expense as selectman,   130.79

Bradford Electric Lighting Co., lighting,   6.00

E. M. Clark, services as supervisor,   46.00

Bradford Electric Lighting Co., lighting 2 months,   12.00

The Woodsville News, printing tax notices,   1.25

W. F. Whitcher, printing check lists,   6.30

Orders drawn:

Bradford Electric Lighting Co., lighting,	$6.00
Bradford Electric Lighting Co., lighting,	6.00
W. W. Coburn, services as supervisor,	15.00
C. S. Newell, on account collector's salary,	300.00
Bradford Electric Lighting Co., lighting to February 1,	15.12
A. F. Kimball, recording vital statistics,	49.50
A. F. Kimball, services as town clerk and telephone rent,	118.00
Raymond U. Smith, legal services,	6.50
Fred S. Wright, legal services,	152.24
C. S. Newell, balance services as collector,	400.00
L. M. Kimball, services as treasurer,	75.00
D. L. Hawkins, services and expenses as selectman,	175.00
H. W. Keyes, services and expenses as selectman,	85.00
W. J. Clough, services and expenses as selectman,	248.96
W. J. Clough, expenses as secretary, postage, telephone and telegraph,	7.24

$2,179.91

Woodsville Fire District

Appropriations:

Raised at district meeting,	$5,150.00	
Proportion of $5000 raised at town meeting,	2,398.85	
		$7,548.85

Orders drawn:

F. L. Sargent,	$500.00	
F. L. Sargent,	500.00	
F. L. Sargent,	1,500.00	
F. L. Sargent,	2,000.00	
F. L. Sargent,	3,048.85	
		$7,548.85

Town School District

Appropriations:

Raised at district school meeting,	$9,650.00	
Proportion of literary fund,	257.39	
Porportion of dog license fund,	241.91	
Proportion of Southard fund,	80.61	
Proportion of state school fund,	1,073.85	
		$11,303.76

Orders drawn:

W. H. Langmaid,	$1,000.00	
W. H. Langmaid,	1,500.00	
W. H. Langmaid,	1,000.00	
W. H. Langmaid,	5,000.00	
W. H. Langmaid,	2,803.76	
		$11,303.76

WOODSVILLE HIGH SCHOOL DISTRICT

Appropriations:

Raised at district school meeting,	$7,620.00	
Proportion of literary fund,	240.79	
Proportion of dog license fund,	226.31	
Proportion of Southard fund,	83.39	
Proportion of state school fund,	900.00	
		$9,070.49

Orders drawn:

F. L. Sargent,	$1,000.00	
F. L. Sargent,	500.00	
F. L. Sargent,	1,000.00	
F. L. Sargent,	2,000.00	
F. L. Sargent,	4,570.49	
		$9,070.49

WATER TROUGHS

No appropriation.

Joseph Henderson,	$3.00
J. M. Butson,	3.00
W. Keith,	3.00
I. A. Lindsey,	3.00
Tyler Westgate,	3.00
Pike Mfg. Co.,	9.00
C. J. Pike estate,	3.00
Lewis Lavoie,	3.00
H. D. Gannett,	3.00
Solomon Newell,	3.00
V. P. Dailey,	3.00

Willis Kelley,
C. M. Kimball,
F. M. Wells,
Charles Bodette,
Woodsville Aqueduct Co.,
Betsey St. Clair,
F. P. Wells,
Robert Butson,
B. M. White,
Charles Burt,
Frank R. Wright,
H. F. Dearborn,
J. R. Day,
Lucy L. Jewett,

Town Poor

There were no paupers chargeable to the to
past year.

QUARANTINE

No appropriation.

S. K. Dearborn, services for Wade Lane,	$6.00
P. W. Allen, on account services as health officer,	25.00
E. B. Mann & Co., supplies for Board of Health,	42.80
Geo. H. Clark, supplies for Board of Health,	30.00
C. H. Johnson, services and expenses as health officer,	91.00
F. M. Astle, supplies for Joe Bedard while under quarantine,	16.72
S. D. McAllister, rent and board for Griffin while under quarantine,	50.00
W. E. Lawrence, attendance Mina Drown, during quarantine,	7.00
Ezra B. Willoughby, services and expenses as health officer,	46.35
Pike Station Store Co., supplies for Gibson during quarantine,	21.84
Pike Provision Co., supplies for Gibson during quarantine,	6.86
F. J. Drury, medical attendance for Gibson,	6.00
Chas. A. Robinson, milk for Gibson during quarantine,	1.95
Henry C. Stearns, medical attendance for Gibson during quarantine,	18.00
P. W. Allen, balance services and expenses as health officer,	44.39

$413.91

HAVERHILL PRECINCT—LIGHTING

Raised at district meeting,		$600.00
Orders drawn:		
J. G. Shepard,	$100.00	
J. G. Shepard,	50.00	
J. G. Shepard,	50.00	
J. G. Shepard,	50.00	
J. G. Shepard,	50.00	
J. G. Shepard,	100.00	
J. G. Shepard,	50.00	
J. G. Shepard,	50.00	
J. G. Shepard,	50.00	
J. G. Shepard,	50.00	
		$600.00

COUNTY POOR

B. H. White, care of Sarah Tuttle,	$20.00
Mrs. Myra Hutchins, care of Hoit children,	10.00
Helen Weed, rent for John Gilbert,	6.00
H. F. Morrison, care of Hannah Kimball,	16.25
Emily Glover, care of Alvah Moulton,	26.00
Mina Drown, care of Bowen baby,	30.00
Mina Drown, rent for Mrs. Cotton,	21.00
Helen Weed, rent for John Gilbert,	3.00
Myra Hutchins, care of Hoit children,	5.00
F. J. Drury, medical attendance for John Gilbert,	6.75
P. W. Allen, care of Sarah Tuttle,	10.00
F. M. Astle, supplies for L. J. Sargent,	6.37
Myra Hutchins, care of C. R. Hoit, children,	5.00

H. F. Morrison, care of Hannah Kimball,	$16.25
Emily Glover, care of Alvah Moulton,	26.00
Mina Drown, care of Bowen baby,	24.00
Mary Thomas, care of Jarvis baby,	4.47
Myra Hutchins, care of Hoit children,	5.00
W. H. Page & Sons, supplies for John Gilbert,	92.36
Mina Drown, rent for Mrs. Cotton,	9.00
Mina Drown, care of Bowen baby,	15.00
Myra Hutchins, care of Hoit children,	5.00
Myra Hutchins, care of Hoit children,	5.00
H. F. Morrison, care of Hannah Kimball,	21.25
Emily Glover, care of Alvah Moulton,	26.00
Myra Hutchins, care of Hoit child,	5.00
H. L. Cameron, supplies for A. N. Leach,	12.00
Woodsville Furniture Co., burial of Leach child,	12.75
D. S. Stone, wood for A. N. Leach,	3.50
F. M. Astle, supplies for A. N. Leach,	10.24
F. M. Astle, supplies for A. N. Leach,	3.92
F. M. Astle, supplies for J. L. Lamarre,	20.00
Myra Hutchins, care of Hoit child,	5.00
D. S. Stone, supplies for A. N. Leach,	2.50
H. F. Morrison, care of Hannah Kimball,	16.25
Emily Glover, care of Hannah Kimball,	26.00
Myra Hutchins, care of Hoit child,	5.00
W. H. Page & Son, supplies for Lena Keyes,	27.00
Myra Hutchins, care of Hoit child,	5.00
W. H. Goodwin, wood for Joe Thomas,	5.60
H. D. Gannett, wood for Sarah Tuttle,	6.75
Henry C. Stearns, medical attendance for John Gilbert,	20.25
P. W. Allen, wood for Sarah Tuttle,	3.00
W. H. Page & Son, supplies for Lena Keyes,	43.31
Myra Hutchins, care of Hoit child,	5.00
	$652.77

Miscellaneous

Orders drawn:

W. W. Coburn, Memorial day,	$50.00
L. J. Southard, damage to team,	29.72
W. H. Kimball, painting bridges,	101.75
Detroit Graphite Co., bridge paint,	78.00
L. M. Kimball, interest on town bonds,	300.00
Fred Hall, overpaid tax,	3.22
Detroit Graphite Co., ½ bbl. bridge paint,	37.70
Fred Clough, damage to team on highway,	45.00
L. E. Knights, fighting forest fire,	12.20
L. E. Knights, fighting forest fire,	1.75
W. E. Dearth, fighting forest fire,	88.47
Percy G. Smith, laying out new highway,	6.50
The United Construction Co., 70 per cent. bridge contract price,	5,199.25
E. C. Getchell, concreting,	100.00
W. K. Kimball, painting bridges,	130.25
A. E. Davis, dragging river for unknown body,	5.75
A. E. Davis, dragging river for Rossa Attilia,	16.25
W. R. Wright, tools for state road, 1912,	7.20
N. E. Rutledge, building new road, Terrace Street, Woodsville,	34.00
A. F. Kimball, bounties on hedgehogs,	5.40
Henry J. Talbot, repairing fence on Haverhill Common,	1.75
Florence Thayer, abated tax,	6.40
Florence A. Willoughby, abated tax,	26.24
Carrie A. Towle, overpaid tax,	100.43
Manson F. Young, admr., abated tax,	9.84
W. J. McMeekin, gravel bank,	150.00
J. M. Getchell, 2 guide boards,	8.50
L. M. Kimball, town bonds and interest,	3,300.00
Rhett R. Scruggs, guide board posts,	26.10
Charles E. Cooper, county tax,	3,408.91
The United Construction Co., Haverhil share final bridge payment,	2,228.25

Orders drawn:

The United Construction Co., cement work on bridge approaches and foundation,	$2,162.60
J. Hadley Fullerton, bridge inspection,	186.95
W. H. Ingalls, work on Haverhill-Newbury bridge approaches, .	161.26
W. W. Bailey, work on Haverhill-Newbury bridge approaches,	79.10
Martin H. Clifford, overpaid tax,	.82
Ernest Perkins, overpaid tax,	3.61
F. F. Partridge, work on guide boards,	7.00
J. J. Jesseman, tax abatement for highway repairs,	11.15
Jesseman Granite Co., tax abatement for highway repairs,	8.20
John B. Straw tax abatement,	11.52
Rhett R. Scruggs, Haverhill-Newbury bridge railing,	123.34
E. M. Miller, reporting vital statistics,	8.25
A. F. Kimball, bounties on hedgehogs,	5.60
Horace E. Fine Co., enameled iron signs,	65.10
E. B. Mann, returning burial permits,	6.50
H. C. Stearns, returning vital statistics,	10.50
A. F. Kimball, bounties on hedgehogs,	1.00
Charles S. Newell, tax abatements,	185.15
E. B. Willoughby, interest on trust funds,	98.97
R. T. Bartlett, insurance on town house,	30.00
F. P. Dearth, insurance on town house and tools,	25.00

$18,710.45

STATEMENT OF COST OF HAVERHILL-NEWBURY BRIDGE

No appropriation.

Paid United Construction Co., for bridge,	$7,427.50
United Construction Co., for cement work on bridge approaches and foundation,	2,162.60
J. H. Fullerton, bridge inspection,	186.95
W. H. Ingalls, work on approaches,	161.26
W. W. Bailey, work on approaches,	79.10
Rhett R. Scruggs, iron railing,	123.34
	$10,140.75

The above represents the cost of half the bridge, the other half being borne by the town of Newbury, Vt.

All of the above items are included in miscellaneous account.

TRUST FUNDS

There are in the hands of the selectmen, bequeathed to the town in trust, the following funds:

By Samuel F. Southard for school purposes,	$5,000.00
For care of cemetery lots:	
By John W. Jackson,	$100.00
Franklin Crouch,	500.00
Ida M. Hunt,	300.00
Thomas B. Jackson,	100.00
Charles G. Smith,	200.00
Rebekah E. Webster,	100.00

By A. W. Lyman,	$100.00
Solon H. Baker, for S. C. Jewett lot,	50.00
Solon H. Baker, for H. S. Baker lot,	50.00
Emily H. Garland, for Moses Knight lot,	75.00
Burns H. Pike,	25.00
E. B. Pike, for E. B. Pike lot,	500.00
E. B. Pike, for Pike relatives' lot,	500.00

The income from the Southard fund has been divided between the two school districts as reported in Haverhill School account and Woodsville High School account.

The income from the trust funds for the care of cemetery lots amounting to $98.97 has been paid over to the Board of Cemetery Commissioners, who have been delegated by the selectmen to expend the same.

All of the above trust funds are deposited in the Woodsville Guaranty Savings Bank with the exception of a portion of the Southard fund which is invested in the city of Laconia bonds.

DOG LICENSE FUND

Received from dog licenses,	$525.20	
Received from A. Goostrey, damages for sheep killed by his dog,	13.00	
		$538.20

Orders drawn:		
C. S. Newell, services as dog officer,	$31.00	
Ed Johnson, sheep killed,	23.00	
Geo. Noyes, sheep killed,	20.00	
		74.00
		$464.20

This balance goes to the schools in the town.

Town Libraries

Raised at March meeting,   ·· $300.00
Orders drawn:
    Trustees of Haverhill Public Libra-
        ries, $300.00

Report of Library Trustees

Received of selectmen 1913 appropria-
    tion, $300.00
Paid Woodsville Free Library, $100.00
      Haverhill Free Library,   100.00
      North Haverhill Free Library,   100.00
                                  —————— $300.00

Respectfully submitted,

                 FRED P. DEARTH,
                   Town Library.Trustee.

Report of Tax Collector

Amount committed for collection, $47,598.70
Paid L. M. Kimball, town treasurer, $47,391.84
Sold to town at tax sale,   206.86
                                —————— $47,598.70

Included in the above is the item of abatements, $185.15.

BOARD OF CEMETERY COMMISSIONERS

TREASURER'S REPORT

To balance in treasury February 15, 1913, $310.10
One year's interest of town of Haverhill
   on trust funds,   98.97
                                         ———— $409.07

DISBURSEMENTS

Paid N. A. and G. A. Wheeler, Center
   Haverhill Cemetery, $20.00
   L. L. Willoughby, labor by N. A.
   Wheeler, Horse Meadow Ceme-
   tery,   35.00
   James M. Jeffers, No. 6 Cemetery,   3.00
   E. Bertram Pike, East Haverhill
   Cemetery,   6.50
   N. A. Wheeler, Center Haverhill
   Cemetery,   14.00
   Jesseman Granite Co., Horse
   Meadow Cemetery,   38.50
   Jesseman Granite Co., Horse
   Meadow Cemetery, Crouch lot,   17.00
   Balance cash in treasury,   275.07
                                           ———— $409.07

TRUST FUNDS IN HANDS OF CEMETERY COMMISSIONERS

Mrs. Charles W. Parmalee fund, $100.00
   (Income care Charles Warren lot, East Haverhill Ceme-
   tery.)
George C. Smith fund, $200.00
   (Income care George C. and Anson A. Smith's lots,
   Center Haverhill Cemetery and Haverhill Cemetery.)

Respectfully submitted,

EZRA B. WILLOUGHBY,
Treasurer.

Haverhill Police Court Report

To the Selectmen of the Town of Haverhill;

I submit herewith report of the Haverhill Police Court for the period from February 1, 1913, to July 1, 1913.

Total number of cases brought before the court, 23.

The classification of offenses is as follows:

Aggravated assault,	1
Abandonment of family,	2
Escape from jail,	3
Keeping for sale liquor,	5
Drunkenness,	12

The Haverhill Police Court ceased to exist on June 30, 1913, having been abolished by the Act of the Legislature creating the District Police Courts.

The town of Haverhill is now included in the Police Court for the District of Haverhill, comprising the towns of Haverhill, Orford, Benton, Warren, Monroe and Piermont.

During the period above named the sum of $322.38 has been received for fines and costs and the same paid to the town treasurer.

DEXTER D. DOW,
Justice Haverhill Police Court.

INVENTORY

	April, 1912	April, 1913	April, 1912	April, 1913
Polls,	977	981	$97,700.00	$98,100.00
Horses,	806	694	91,636.00	86,459.00
Mules,	6	5	450.00	375.00
Oxen,	8	12	650.00	915.00
Cows,	1,770	1,717	70,431.50	73,531.00
Other neat stock,	851	517	23,369.00	14,631.00
Sheep,	239	191	1,408.00	852.00
Hogs,	154	90	1,409.00	1,103.00
Fowls,	100		50.00	50.00
Vehicles and Automobiles,	140	173	25,070.00	31,000.00
Portable mills,	1		900.00	700.00
Wood, lumber, etc., not stock in trade,			3,270.00	1,130.00
Stock in public funds,			99,102.00	
Municipal bonds and notes,				61,400.00
Stock in national banks, in this state,			22,898.75	13,895.17
Money on hand, at interest or on deposit,			220,100.02	74,023.73
Stock in trade,			215,057.85	214,312.31
Aqueducts, toll bridges, etc.,			98,600.00	105,150.00
Real estate,			1,830,599.00	1,841,919.00
			$2,802,701.12	*$2,619,546.21
Amount of soldiers' exemption,			24,820.00	
			$2,777,881.12	

* The totals in 1913 were made up deducting the amount exempted to soldiers from each item where the exemption occurred by direction of the State Tax Commission. The total amount of soldiers' exemption for 1913, is $25,595.

Tax Rate

	1912	1913
In Haverhill,	$1.58	$1.64
In Woodsville,	1.85	1.92
In Haverhill Precinct,	1.76	1.85

Financial Statement

LIABILITIES

Town bonds outstanding December 1, 1913,	$12,000.00	
Interest on same to February 16, 1914,	100.00	
Portion of state highway maintenance fund in town treasury,	179.10	
Portion of state highway construction fund in town treasury,	788.09	
Dog license fund 1913–1914,	464.20	
Due Woodsville schools on superintendent's salary,	266.67	
Due Haverhill schools on superintendent's salary,	266.66	
		$14,064.72

ASSETS

Due for rent of town hall,	$18.50
Due from leased land,	96.00
Balance due from Grafton county,	285.32
Due from state treasurer, bounties on hedgehogs,	12.00

Due from abutters, Haverhill,	$196.44	
Taxes bought by town, 1914 sale,	206.86	
Taxes bought by town previous to 1914 sale,	137.47	
Cash in hands of Louis M. Kimball, treasurer,	4,647.76	
		5,600.35

Net indebtedness February 15, 1914,	$8,464.37
Net indebtedness February 16, 1913,	6,069.51

Net increase in debt during the past year,	$2,394.86

There is in the state treasury credited to the Town of Haverhill the following sums:

Permanent highway maintenance fund,	$204.28
State highway construction fund,	2,363.01

These balances will remain in the state treasury for future expenditures in the town.

Respectfully submitted,

HENRY W. KEYES,
WILLIAM J. CLOUGH,
DEXTER L. HAWKINS,
Selectmen of Haverhill.

AUDITOR'S REPORT

To the Taxpayers of the Town of Haverhill:

Your auditors have examined, in detail, the books and accounts cf the town treasurer, selectmen, and road agents. The books are correctly kept, the accounts vouched, and the reports as prepared for the printer are hereby approved. The various trust funds are as reported, intact, and properly invested. All unexpended balances of the income of these funds have been added to their respective funds, and each fund is now kept in every sense distinct and separate.

Cash and securities belonging to the town are intact as reported.

In our presence and that of the town treasurer, town bonds numbered 43, 44 and 45, each of the denomination of one thousand dollars ($1,000) also coupons numbered 29 and 30 due on all outstanding bonds amounting to six hundred dollars ($600) we destroyed by burning.

WILLIAM F. WHITCHER,
NORMAN J. PAGE,
Auditors.

VITAL STATISTICS

VITAL STATISTICS.

To THE SELECTMEN OF HAVERHILL: In ... ce with an act of the Legislature ... ed June session, 1877, ... ing "clerks of ... and cities to furnish a transcript of births, ... ings and deaths to the ... ors for publication in the ... al reports,"
I ... hit the following:

BIRTHS REGISTERED IN THE TOWN OF HAVERHILL FOR THE YEAR ENDING DECEMBER 31, 1913.

Date of birth.	Name of the child (if any).	Sex.	Living or stillborn.	No. of child.	Name of father.	Maiden name of mother.	Occupation of father.	Birthplace of father.	Birthplace of mother.
1911. Dec. 26	Kenneth Whittemore	M	L	1	Edward ... We	... rie Dushane	R. R. employee	Lawrence, Mass.	... er., Ms.
1912. Feb. 5	Jeph ... Two	M	L	3	N ... rola Frisco	Ba Di ... Mo.	Laborer	... k.	Italy.
Nov. 26	... form ... e ... g	F	L	3	N ... nnn J. Page	Helen R. ... Me.	Supt. of Schools	Benton	Pawtucket, R. I.
Dec. 4	Francis Keyes[1]	M	L	3	H ... nry W. Keyes	Fas P. ... Mr.	Farmer	... by, Vt.	... lle, V.
1913. Jan. 5	Robert White	M	L	4	... ster ... Wte	Nel ... Mass	... engineer	... reda	... thd, Vt.
14	Edna ... Mon ... Ri	F	L	2	... Mil Keith	Lilla B. ... White	... fiher	...	... hn.
20	Ida Odell Dargie	F	L	5	Peter Dargie	Rosie Boulieu	... e ... ter	... "	... da.
29	Vincent Charles Kimball	M	L	2	Ray E. Kimball	Della E. ... ole	... o ... plee	... ter	Averill, Vt.
Feb. 4	... Guyette	M	L	5	... d A. ... uyette	Me G. White	... er	... ld	... da.
10	Bert Robinson ... Ghee	F	L	2	... y Robinson	Me E. H bbs	Farmer	Lyme	Haverhill.
12	Marion Elizabeth ... Ghee	F	L	3	Milo ... Ghee	Emily E. ... Hbns	Boiler ... r	... ter	England
15	... Winnie	M	L	2	L. L. Winnie	Adella ... Me	R. R. ... rfian	... ter	Union City, Conn.
17	Claude Simson White	F	L	2	Fred A. ... We	Florence ... Hard	... ror	... ton, N. Y.	Dalton.
17	... lle Harrison Pii ... e[2]	M	L	...	E. ... sin ... Bie.	Mamie Pearson	Eng. house ... n	Haverhill	... ham, Md
24	... Me ... use Campbell	F	L	2	Fred R. Campbell	Fannie ... Whan	Fireman	Salem, Ms.	... da.
24	1 ... Be ... ph Lavoie	M	L	4	John Lavoie	Albertina De Lisle	Stone ... utter	Groton, Vt.	... by, Vt.
24	Edward ... des Cornell	M	L	1	... chd B. ... Gell	Lillian G. ... Hdes	... ller	Walcott, Vt.	... Mn.
March 2	... nell ... Tyr	M	L	2	Ira W. Thayer	Hattie ... Mn	Lawyer	Bath	... thn., Md.
5	Edgar Davison Sargent	M	L	6	Lemuel ... gt	... aby J. Leach.	Farmer	Eden, Vt.	Haverhill.

[1] b. Boston, Mass.   [2] b.   ... Mn, Mass.

Date	No.	Name of Child	Sex		Name of Father	Name of Mother	Occupation	Residence	Birthplace
March 13		———	M	L	Wk Sequin.	Freda Ti ?in	Drug clerk.	?v Point, N. Y.	U ?ill, Vt.
April 1	1	?nd	M	L	Wm R. Atwood.	?in Ray ?y.	R. R. station agent.	Rumney.	Rumney.
3	2	Hn ?ay	M	L	Mo J.	?er ?y.	Laborer.	Haverhill.	?ld, Vt.
7	2	?a	F	L	Harry " "	?l C. Heath.	Clerk.	?, Vt.	?ld, Vt.
7	3	?e	F	L					" "
11	6	—Cookman	M	L	Albert ?n.	My Lancaster.	Laborer.	?a.	Canada.
14	2	?n L?e Hill.	F	L	Oscar E. Hall.	?e M. Foster.	Clk in store.	?nt.	Wentworth.
15	2	Ge ?n	F	L	Selwyn K. Dearborn.	?e ?is.	?ician.	Bristol.	Strafford.
15	1	?ia ?ee	M	L		?ay ?s Barney.	?ight checker.	?a.	Lancaster.
18	3	?in Lewis ?in.	M	L	Lewis Nelson.	?a ?s.	Farmer.	Waitesfield, Vt.	Haverhill.
20	2	Lawrence Stephen Travena	M	L	Stephen E. ?ea.	?e C. Lewis.	" "	Lyman.	?nn.
May 3	4	?h William Ladeau	F	L	?h W. Ladeau.	Ida A.	R. R. Employee	Mn, Vt.	?y, ?.
9	3	?a My ?	F	L	?d S. ? Mn.	?ee My ?	R. R. ?pl ?ye.	Groveton.	?ally, ?.
11	3	Pauline Smith.	F	L	Silas Hurlbutt.	?fo ?itt.	Laborer.	?ill.	?ill.
11	1	?a Drusella	M	L	Ray Bailey	Jenniss Mitchell	R. R. employee.	Durham.	?nn.
12	3	Viola Elizabeth Hurlbutt.	F	L	?in E. White.	?e M. Lamere	Box ?ker	?n.	"
24	1	Marjorie Lura Bailey	F	L	?nk H. Keith.	?e M. Gonyer.	Farmer.	Groton.	Irasburg, Vt.
27	3	Vincent C. White.	F	L	David F. ?e.	?e B. ?ith.	?n.	Canada.	Haverhill.
29	1	?	M	L	?h Sutherland.	Julie E. Kimball.	R. R. employee.	?ill	N ?by, Vt.
June 3	3	Dulsie June ?te.	F	L	?h W Rogers	?is May Clough.	Farmer.	?ill, Vt.	Marlboro, M.
4	1	?ald ?aie	M	L	William O. Hunt.	?e A. ?er	R. R. employee.	Salem, Mass.	?h.
10	3	?er Sara ?nt.	F	L	George H. Hood.	?a Crosby.	Farmer.	Lancaster.	Concord.
16	5	Lovia ?a Spinney	F	L	Vernon W. Smith.	Sarah Perkins	R. R. engineer	Nova ?a.	Bath.
uly 1	4	?in E. Hood.	M	L	Charles J. O'Neil.	?yl Sawyer	R. R. employee.	?l ?us Falls, Vt.	Littleton.
3	2	?oll Richard ?ith.	F	L	George W. French.	Florence E.	Dry goods clerk.	Orford.	Lisbon.
5	2	?lin ?nes O'Neil.	M	L	Perley E. ?d.	?ne M. O'Conner.	Farmer.	Warren.	Keene.
5	1	My Velha ?n.	M	L	George H. N ?s.	Lutheria ?ith.	?g clerk.	Me.	Barnet, Vt.
18	6	?in Lawrence French.	M	S		Florence Smith.	Farmer.	Haverhill.	Concord, ?.
20	5	Ned	F	L		Corah Danforth	" "	Haverhill.	Bradford, Vt.
21	1	?w Wilson	F	L		?la Danforth	" "	Tr ?y ?Vt.	Haverhill.
25	11	——Boardman.	M	L		My Brown.	" "	G ?y, N. Y.	Orford.
27	3	Emily B. Wise.	M	L	John W. Wise.	?a Barker.	Physician.	Haverhill.	Northville, N. Y.
Aug. 8		Martha Elizabeth True.	F	L	Charles ?ld.	?z A. Briggs	?ith.	McIndoes, Vt.	Ayer, M.
15		?ith ?e ?ld.	F	L	?rt P. ?McttrIck	Bertha A. ?e.	?ith.	?ill.	?ill
24		?d McYettrick	M	L	?ry F. Dearborn.	Maude Green	Farmer.	Newbury, Vt.	Newbury, Vt.
30		Myl ?e Dearborn.	M	L	Hiram A. ?by	Grace L. ?ier	R. R. ?mployee	Lancaster.	Haverhill.
21		Gladys M. Derby	M	L	Asa S. ?vt.	Cora Leonard	?er	?ill.	Glover, ?.
Oct. 3		Leonard Kimball Prescott.	M	L	Henry G. Scruggs	Bertha E.	?er.	?er.	Haverhill.
3		Beverly ?e Scruggs	F	L	?ed Sawyer	Mary Adams.	?ir	?b ?s, S. C.	?nn, M.
7		—— Sawyer.	M	L	Benjamin Evans	N ?he ?s.	Farmer.	N ?by, Vt.	Henniker.
22		Gerald ?lter ?e.	M	L	?n E. St ?	Mariam Simpson	" "	?ith.	Haverhill.
25		Althea Nelson.	F	L	Ernest W. Nelson.	Eva Wheeler.		Haverhill.	Haverhill.

BIRTHS REGISTERED IN THE TOWN OF HAVERHILL FOR THE YEAR ENDING DECEMBER 31, 1913—Concluded.

Date of birth.	Name of the child (if any).	Sex.	Living or stillborn.	No. of child.	Name of father.	Maiden name of mother.	Occupation of father.	Birthplace of father.	Birthplace of mother.
Oct. 27	Ellis Hazel MacD.	F	L	1	Finley MacDonald	Isabel Polk	Electrician	Scotland	Haverhill.
Nov. 12	Dorothy Edna Ada Robinson	F	L	3	Charles A. Robinson	Lea Tondro	Farmer	England	England.
13	Edith Maud Jackwood	M	L	2	Richard J. Jackwood	Eva S. Keyes	"	Newark, N. J.	Haverhill.
14	James Alfred Downing	M	L	1	Charles David Downing	Delia ———	"	Ireland.	Ireland.
21	Ruth Kimball Prescott	F	L	1	Ernest K. Prescott	Ruth Ainsworth	Railroading	Lunenburg, Vt.	Elmre, Vt.
26	Richard Oris Emerson	M	L	2	Lawrence Emerson	Althea Doll	Whetstone finisher	Gilby, Vt.	Nova Scotia.
29	—— Obrien	M	L	4	Matew J. Obrien	Ella M. Hartigan	Baker	Dover.	Rochester.
29	Iva Orrill Heath	M	L	4	Arthur A. Heath	Matilda M. Danforth	Butter maker	Bradford, Vt.	Bath.
29	Iva Matilda Heath	F	L	5	" "	"	"	"	"
7	Willard White Atkins	M	L	4	Willard G. Atkins	Ruth E. Webb	Merchant	Woodbury, Vt.	Jericho, Vt.
10	Mariannino Frisco	M	L	4	Nila Frisco	Rosa Di Mico	Roundabout	Italy	Italy.
11	Catherine Stokes	F	L	5	Charles Stokes	Hattie Dargneau	Laborer	Mass. Vt.	Canada.
14	Ralph Lougee Reed	M	L	2	Ralph H. Reed	Lena Thurston	Farmer	Bath	Hartford, Vt.

All unless otherwise indicated born in Haverhill.

I hereby certify that the foregoing return is correct, according to the best of my knowledge and belief.

A. F. KIMBALL, *Town Clerk.*

MARRIAGES RE—GISTERED IN THE TOWN OF HAVERHILL FOR THE YEAR ENDING DECEMBER 31, 1913.

Date of Marriage.	Place of marriage.	Name and surname of groom and bride.	Residence of each at time of marriage.	Age.	Occupation of groom and bride.	Place of birth of each.	Names of parents.	Place of parents.	Occupation.	Marriage.	Name, date and official station of person by whom married.
1913. Jan. 7	Haverhill	Bron Royston	Haverhill	30	Teller	So. Troy, Vt.	William Royston	Canada	Liveryman	1	Alba M. May, North Haverhill.
		Nellie May White	"	20	Housework	Hyde Park, Vt.	Mary O'Heas		Housewife	2 D	Jogan
11	Littleton	Fred B. Lang	"	52	Lawyer	Bath	John Vancor, Della Eng	Bath	Farmer	3 DD	George G. ams, Mh.
		Ethel X. Wills	Mon	21	Stenographer	Littleton	James Lang, Ean Parker	Littleton	Housewife	1	gel
18	Haverhill	Ua W. Brockway	West Burke, Vt.	52	Merchant	Sutton, Vt.	Edwin E. Wills, nale A. Perkins	Boundry Line, Vt.	Blacksmith	3 WD	C. F. McIntire, Woodsville.
		Me Ron	"	35	Teller	Burke, Vt.	Josiah Brockway, Fhebe Rider	San, Vt.	Wheelwright	1	Clergyman.
20	"	Thomas A. Carr	May, Vt.	36	Quarryman	anda	Ban Ron, Joseph Gr	Burke, Vt.	Farmer	2 D	Alba M. kM, North Haverhill
		Bertha W. Brown	Montpelier, Vt.	42	Housework	Adt, Vt.	Jennie Atkinson	neda	Housewife	2 W	Farmer
Feb. 1	"	Lewis W. Nelson	Haverhill	27	Laborer	Md, Vt.	Henry McLoud, Emily A. Andrews	Adamant, Vt.	Quarryman	1	Alba M. Markey, North Haverhill.
		Emma M s a o	"	16	Housework	Haverhill	Ida 1 My, oMe W. Mon	Fayston, Vt.	Housewife	1	gel
M. 4	Lyman	Edge J. Blake	"	26	Carpenter	Als, Vt.	Sylvanus Mes, Emma Lamont	Tunbridge, Vt.	Basket maker	2D	C. L. Corliss, Lisbon.
		Edith B. Clough	Lyman	27	Nurse	Lyman	Tim M. Blake, Mary A. Slayton	Burlington, Vt.	Carpenter	1	gel
10	Haverhill	Fred C. Perry	Prt, Vt.	30	R. R. emp.	Lige, Vt.	Durb L. Clough, Mary F. gt	Lowell, Vt.	Blacksmith	2 D	L. R. Dsfth, Wile.
		Mbel M. ofge	Derby, Vt.	26	Housework	Canada	Darius Perry, Ellen Greggs	As, Vt.	Housewife	2 D	gel
11	"	Leon F. Wire	Haverhill	23	Mh. helper	M	Ada ane La Foe, Frank D. We	nhin, Vt.	Farmer	1	C. F. Mre, Wile.
		Mabel Nelson	"	23	Housework	Haverhill	Lilla Hubbard, Stephen Plant, Dell M. Tibbetts	Dalton, Shelburne, Vt. aeda	Retired, Mach. helper, Housework, Farmer, Housework	2 W	gel

MARRIAGES REGISTERED IN THE TOWN OF HAVERHILL FOR THE YEAR ENDING DECEMBER 31, 1913.—C ? add.

Date of Marriage.	Place of marriage.	Name and name of groom and bride.	Residence of each at time of marriage.	Age.	Occupation of groom and bride.	Place of birth of each.	Names of parents.	Place of parents.		Marriage.	Name, and official station of pen by whom married.
Mar. 13	Haverhill	Timothy S. Bartlett	Newbury, Vt.	65	Jobber	Newbury, Vt.	Julie C. Danforth	Newbury, Vt.	Farmer	2 W	C. F. ... Woodsville.
		Emma Hadlock	Haverhill	27	Clerk	Haverhill	Joseph Hadlock	"	Housewife / Laborer	1	Clergyman.
17	Lakeport	Percy Derusha	"	20	R. R. emp.	Littleton	Joseph Derusha	Newbury, Vt.	Housewife.	1	E. B. Young, Lakeport.
		Lulia May Leland	"	18	Housework	Newbury, Vt.	Jennie Virtue. / William P. Leland	Canada.	R. R. emp. / Housewife.	1	
Apr. 14	Haverhill	Frederick Morrill	"	21	Mail carrier	WhiteRock, R.I.	Mary A. Cross. / Eben Morrill	Derby, Vt.	R. R. emp. / Mail carr	1	John Hold Haverhill.
		Beulah Helen Brown	"	18	Housework	Haverhill	Nancy Holt. / Allen M. Brown	Sutton, Mass.	Housewife. / Farmer.	1	Clergyman.
19	"	Benj. F. King	Derby, Vt.	18	Clerk	Newbury, Vt.	Lizzie Titus. / Giles H. Deming	Haverhill	Housewife. / Granite deal'r	1	C. F. ... Woodsville.
		Ruth K. Lowe	"	18	Student	Montpelier, Vt.	Vail / Wilbur O. Lowe	Montpelier, Vt.	Housewife. / Clerk.	1	Clergyman.
21	"	Edwin Herbert Bartlett	Haverhill	30	R. R. clerk.	Bethlehem	Kate / Walter E. Bartlett	Easton	Housewife. / Farmer.	1	C. F. ...
		Ella Lula Matthews	"	30	Saleswoman.	Concord, Vt.	Helen W. ... / Stephen M. Matthews	...ford, Vt.	Housewife. / Station agent	1	y ...
24	Littleton	Hugh M. Dearborn	"	21	Clerk	Plymouth.	Alice E. Gilbert. / Henry L. Dearborn	Plymouth.	Housewife. / R. R. cond.	1	William A. ...
		Mildred McClintock	Lisbon.	20	Housework	Lisbon.	Jennie L. Gerrish / David ...	North.	Housewife. / Farmer.	1	Clergyman.
May 1	Haverhill	John C. Sherburne	Randolph, Vt.	29	Lawyer.	Pomfret, Vt.	Effie Spooner / John C. ...	Lisbon.	Housewife. / Farmer.	1	Homer White, Randolph, Vt.
		Alice C. ...	"	27	Librarian	Randolph, V.	William E. Giddings / Benj. G. McIntyre	Pomfret, Vt.	Housewife. / Business mgr.	1	Clergyman.
5	"	Lawrence Emerson	Haverhill	40	finisher.	Derby, Vt.	Rosabelle Bradford / Daniel Emerson	Barre, Vt.	Housewife. / Farmer.	2 D	A. F. Kimball, North Haverhill.
		Althea Dall	"	27	Housework.	Nova Scotia.	Hannah Corliss / Silas Dall / Hattie	Nova Scotia.	Housewife.	1	Justice of the Peace.

Date	Place	Name	Age	Occupation	Birthplace	Parents	Residence	No.	By whom married
May 7	Haverhill	Leroy L. ... Mn.	28	Laborer	Manchester	... A. McQuesten / ... Jull	Manchester	1	J. Roy Dinsmore, Me. Carpenter
		Gladdies M. Hobbs	24	Housework	Haverhill	John L. Hobbs / Bessie L. Nas a	Warren	1	Clergyman. Housewife Farmer
Jne 4	Laconia	Harry E. Griffin	27	R. R. emp	Canada	Charles F. Griffin / Jane Swift	Gorham	1	Arthur M. Slk, Laconia. Farmer
		Blanche L. Austin	25	Clerk	No. Troy, Vt.	Alonzo Austin / aura Ward	Canada	1	Clergyman. Housewife
11	Haverhill	Wesley ... Mes	21	Farmer	Haverhill	Sylvanus Mes / ... Jeme	Richford, Vt. / Enosburgh, Vt.	1	Arthur H. Drury, East Haverhill. Farmer
		Alice Young	43	Housewife		Ira Swain / Alma Glazier	Tunbridge, Vt. / Royalton, Vt.	2 W	Clergyman. Housewife
18	"	Wm H. J lin	19	Freight h	Whitefield	Henry Jln / Phebe Goslin	Warren	1	J. R. Dinsmore, Me. Carpenter Retired
	"	Flra M. Non	18	Housework		George W. Nelson / Hattie Webster	Haverhill	1	Clergyman. Housewife
21	Plymouth	Cl ence Henry Andrews	24	Laborer	Laconia	Fred G. Andrews / Orra ...	Canada	1	Albert L. Smith, Plymouth. Farmer
		Esther L. ...	20	...er	Haverhill	Samuel Hildreth / Emma L. Andrews	Lyme	1	Clergyman. Laborer Housewife
25	Boston, Mass.	Daniel Carr	29	Farmer	"	Daniel E. Carr / Ida M. Carr	Bath	1	David McDonald, Boston, Mass. Farmer
		Sadie A. Reeves	25	Teacher	Charlestown, Mass.	Edwin B. Reeves / el L. Brooks	Boston, Mass. / Haverhill	1	Clergyman. Housewife
29	Concord	Earl C. Whittier	24	Brakeman	Haverhill	Henry H. Whittier / Dora Babb	Jefferson, Me. / Calais, Me.	1	George H. Reed. Concord. Retired Housewife
		Eva May Sawyer	25	...	Concord	Charles W. Sawyer / ia Marston	Bath	1	Baker Housewife
July 15	Haverhill	Franklin F. Reams	28	Millwright	Easton, Mass.	B F. Reams / Mia H. Gifford	Benton / Philadelphia, Pa.	1	Thomas edden, H Me. Carpenter Housewife
	"	Era Duprat	37	Dressmaker	Winooski, Vt.	Why Duprat / Flavie Langlois	Dartmouth, Mass.	1	Priest. Carpenter Dressmaker
16	"	mer E. Applebee	45	Farmer	Haverhill	George Aee / Mary Ingerson	Carroll	2 W	A. F. Kimball, North Haverhill Carpenter Dressmaker Farmer
		B rtha dey	18	Housework	Bath	Charles Corey / Mattie Hill	Jefferson	1	J. P. Housewife
30	Littleton	Pearley W. Carpenter	28	Laborer	Littleton	William T. / Emma Shepard	Morrisville, Vt.	1	J. Harry LeRoy, Littleton. Housework Laborer
		Minnie E. Cutti g	24	Housework	Haverhill	Geo. F. Cutting / Emma A. Sherwell	Haverhill	3 W D	Clergyman. Housewife Farmer
ug. 12	Haverhill	Edward W. no	45	Painter	Bethel, Vt.	Alexus no / Adeline W. Willey	St. ... Vt.	1	C. H. Hosford, Me. Housewife Wheelwright
	"	Lillian E. Demings	38	Housework	White River Junction, Vt.	Strong / Belle Strong		2 W	J. P. Housewife

MARRIAGES REGI   IN THE TOWN OF HAVERHILL FOR THE YEAR ENDING DECE   ER 31, 1912.—*Concl   d.*

Date of Marriage.	Place of marriage.	Name and surname of groom and bride.	of each at time of marriage.	Age.	of groom and bride.	Place of birth of each.	of parents.	Birthplace of parents.	of .	Marriage.	and official station of person by whom married.
Aug. 13	Haverhill		, Vt.	21	Laborer	, Vt.	Murdo Graham	Scotland		1	J. R. Dinsmore, Me.
		Lilla	"	21	Housework	"	Lilla	, Vt.	Housewife	1	Me.
18	"	Arthur E.	Haverhill	52	Dep. sheriff	Bd, Vt.	Gustie	e, Vt.	Housewife	2 D	J. R. Me.
		le S.	"	42	H useworko.	Haverhill	Nelson S. Handford	th, "	Farmer	2 D	y n. Me.
21	"	Edward A.	"	23	Boiler	Whitefield.	Joseph A.	Haverhill		1	A. M. Markey, North Haverhill.
		Gertrude M.	"	25	Waitress	Canada.	Clara Jolin	Canada.	Housewife	2 D	y n.
Sept. 9	"	Samuel A.	"	50	Farmer	, Vt.	Mina	, Vt.	Farmer	2 D	A. M. Markey, Nrth Haverhill.
		r Farr.	Cabot, Vt.	43	Housework	Cabot, Vt.	Smith	er, Vt.	Housewife	2 D	y n.
13	"	on L. Scott	Boston, Ms.	25	Student	St. is, M.	Robert D. Scott	, Mass.	Lawyer	1	J. R.
			Nw rk, N.Y.	24	Artist		E. Rexford	, Ark.	Housework.	1	Me.
27	"	Carl Aln Yorke	Wells, Me.	23	Carpenter	Boston, Ms.	Alvin Yorke	Charleston, Vt.	Real est. agt.	1	J. R. ore, Me.
		Mud Hardison	Berwick, Me.	19		Berwick, Me.	Burt Hardison	Me.	Housewife	1	n. Me.
30	"	Wen C. Howland	Brandon, Vt.	33	Farmer	Goshen, Vt.	Addie Gove	Berwick, Me.	She Cutter	1	ob Fuller, Haverhill.
		ha A. Holmes	, Vt.	24	Housework	der, o.	Edward Howland	Brandon, Vt.	Sawyer	1	y n.
Oct. 13	"	s Barber	Haverhill	38	Farmer	England	Clark Holmes		Farmer	3 DW	Alba M. Markey, th Haverhill.
		Ada May	"	30	Housework	Orford	W. H. Gilman	England	Housewife	2 W	y n.
							Clara B. Veasey	Bradford, Vt.	Housework		

Date	Residence	Name	Age	Occupation	Birthplace	Parents	No.	Officiant
Oct. 15	Haverhill	Sidney W. Humphrey	25	Coal dealer	Lawrence, Mass	Edward H. Humphrey	1	Arthur H. Drury, East Haverhill.
	"	Katherine Pike	"	Housewife	Lawrence, Mass	Susan ... H. Pike	1	Clergyman.
			27	Stenographer	Haverhill	Eliza A. French	1	G. N. Dorr, Lancaster.
Nov. 5	Lancaster	Mr Howard Learned	29	B. & M. host'r	Lancaster	Willis ...	1	Clergyman.
	Lancaster	Mary Alice ...	24	Housework	Bethlehem	Laura Cutti ...	1	C. F. McIntire, Woodsville.
18	Haverhill	Carl Lionel Smyth	19	Baggage ...	Laconia	Minnie Smith	1	Clergyman.
	"	Pearl Berma Smith	20	Milliner and dressmaker	Horton, Iowa	Frank Smith	1	W. F. Whitcher, ...ville.
22	"	Maurice Fred Varney	23	R. R. ...	Bethlehem	Lena B. Davis	1	J. P.
	Whitefield	Jennie Smith	20	Housework	Whitefield	Alfred ...	1	A. M. Markey, North Haverhill.
Dec. 10	Haverhill	Frederick Timothy Clough	23	Farmer	Haverhill	Mary Brooks	1	Clergyman.
	"	Eva May Wells	23	Teacher	"	Fred Varney	1	A. H. Drury, East Haverhill.
24	"	Mge Martin Thmpson	24	Whetstone grinder	Portsmouth	Alice McKee	1	Clergyman.
	"	Mary Olive Mer	18	Housework	Portland, Me.	Lucius F. ...		

I hereby certify that the above return i ...spect, ...ording to the best of my n...wledge and belief.

A. F. KIMBALL, *Town Clerk.*

DEATHS REGI[STERED] IN THE TOWN OF HAVERHILL FOR THE YEAR ENDING DECEMBER 31, 1913.

Date of death	Name and surname of the deceased	Years	Months	Days	Place of birth	Sex	Sing., mar., or widow.	Occupation	Name of father	Maiden name of mother	Disease or cause of death
Jan. 18	Laura M. Mason	81	6	22	Haverhill	F	W	Housewife	Samuel Carr	Elizabeth Brewster	Aortic sclerosis.
21	Willie E. [M]on	55	1	7	Orford	M	M	Carpenter	Daniel Y. Simpson	[Mtha]	Pernicious ana[emia].
27	Helen Rumsey	85	5	16	[?], Vt.	F	W	Housewife	Turel C. [Martin]	Betsy Cason	[Hear]t disease of heart.
Feb. 3	Hattie F. Smith	67	11	28	Haverhill	F	W	"	John G. White	Susan Sanborn	Anemia.
12	[M]in S. [Mar]	63	2	12	[Mr.]	M	M		Paul N. Meader [J.]		[ulc]er of stomach.
13	Ella Jane (Leslie) Graves	61	9	10	Newbury, Vt.	F	W	Housewife	George R. [Leslie]		[de]bility.
15	Adeline M. Cooley	91	9	3	[?]in.	F	W	"	Daniel Wilson	Rebecca	Senile debility.
24	Edward J. [M]s	48	8	16	Fairfield, Vt.	M	M	Farmer	[Hfas] [Mrris]	Mary Burke	Apoplexy.
26	Baby Campbell			2	Haverhill	F	S		Fred R. [Campbell]	[annie] [Man]	[Min].
28	Amy T[i]	58		1	Bath	F	M	Housewife	[any] [til]	[GMnia] [Wrd]	Pneumonia.
Mar. 4	[M]a A. [M]son	58	11	5	Hanover	M	S		Earl Wheeler	[afre] Larkin	[cate] ([?].
5	C [alre] [Witer]	25			Hanover	F	M	Housewife	[Mes] [Awod], Jr.	[dnda] Smith	Miscarriage.
9	[Kia] Barita	87			Italy	F	W	"	James Larkin	N [llie] o [Gahell]	Broken leg.
15	Clarence W. [May]	47	2	18	Haverhill, Vt.	M	S	Painter	[John] [Mnde]	Mary [My]	[Wdar ... sese of] chrt.
25	[aMes] B. Harriman	1	9	18	Haverhill	M	S		Henry Harriman	[Ade] G. Harriman	[Mra] infantum.
Apr. 5	Harry Tallman		4	9	Boston, Mass.	M	S		[Mer] [Man]	[Alea] Dall	Broncho-pneumonia.
15	Alice [odes] [Milby]	62	8	22	Northfield, Vt.	F	W	Boarding house.	Horace Jones	Roxana Page	Pneumonia.
16	Lois F. Fisher	69			Haverhill	F	D		Horatio [Pge]	Carolyne Bailey	Bright's disease.
23	Grace [aMon]	1		5		F	S		S. K. [?]	[add] Johnson	[n] [fatal] heart disease.
May 22	[age] C. Jeffers	79	7	7		M	M	Farmer	[Isaah] Jeffers	[Ldia] [Gn]	Sarcoma.
29	Ralph [Men]	18	7	8		M	S	Student	[Joseph] N.	[adde] Coburn	[Ma] of [artis].
June 3	[aMel] [Le]	45	5	4	Bath	M	M	[Clk]	Horace [?]	Marcia White	Marasmus.
21	[age] G. [Le]		4		Haverhill	M	S		Edward [ute]	Mary White	Senile debility.
27	Phebe [Me]	78	1	14	Bath	F	W	Housewife	Horace Battis	Betsy Rix	Cerebral.
27	Wilbur F. [Rasan]	61	8	7	Haverhill	M	M	Farmer	Hubert Eastman	Esther [Ra]	Drowned.
	[atilia] Rosi	27			Italy	F	S	Laborer	[Gppi] Rosi	[Gah] Sutherland	Spina bifida.
July 9	Donald L.			24	Haverhill	M	S		Fred [?]	Alice Carter	Shock [used] by [?].
21	Gllys Elsie [utler] / Fred Hill	2 / 61	9 / 3	25 / 29	[?]	F / M	S / M		Joseph Hill	Eva V. Skinner / Zoe Dubuc	[Pbic] Carcinoma.

Month	Day	Name	Yr	Mo	Da	Place of Birth	Sex	Cond.	Occupation	Father	Mother	Cause of Death
July	23	Isaiah A. Day	60	11	7	Haverhill	M	S	Farmer	... W. Day	Hannah B.	Cholelit...
	24	Philomen Oakes	75	5	22	Haverhill	M	W	"	Francis Oakes	My Ann	Fracture of ...
	27	— Boardman				Haverhill	M	S			My Brown	Stillborn.
Aug.	31	Geo. H. Mann	65	5	12	Benton	M	M	Conductor	G. R.	Susan	Suicide by hanging.
	9	Margaret F. ...	25	3	7	Jay, Mass.	F	M	Housewife	G. W.	Margret	Uraemic coma.
	14	Andy M. White	3	4	18	Haverhill	M			David Frew		...tal burning.
	15	Emily We...			9	Haverhill	F	S	Retired	... W. Pike	Edna Barker	Cardiac insufficiency.
	16	...s J. Pike	66	7	23		M	M	Retired	Drury Pike	...sa Burbank	...
	24	Solomon S. ...iley	82	4	13	Barnet, Vt.	M	M	Farmer	Charles ...iley	Betsy	Diabetis.
	25	...hn G. Olney	67			...da	M	M	Retired			Ilio colitis.
	30	James Burnie					M	S				
Sept.	3	Howard ...	7	8	2	Bethlehem	M	S	Student	J. W.	Emma La Force	Acute ...
	6	Arthur R. ...	24	7	12	"	M	S	R. R. employee	...ry	Isabella McDonald	Burned by steam.
	13	F. W. Hanchett					M	W	Laborer			
	20	John Childs Lang	90	7	5	Bath	M	M	Farmer	William Lang	...tha Childs	Acute cystis...
	20	...an Heath	80	3	13	Haverhill	M	M	"		Harriet Willis	...
	24	George Wheat	58	5	16	Winooski, Vt.	M	M	Switchman			Syncope.
	29	Henry K. Dow	79	10	20	Newbury, Vt.	M	S	Housework	Josiah Dow		... sclerosis.
Oct.	14	Julie R. Carr	64	5	18	...ill	F	S		Samuel ...	— Brewster	Apo...cy.
	22	Viola Bell ...			11		F	S		Wm F. Ford	Hattie F. Weeks	Convulsions.
	25	Frank E. ...ach	2	20			M	S		Allen N. Leach	Nila Cofran	...
Nov.	13	Lois ...Mia Adams	48	11	19	Bath	F	M	Housework	John H. Hamm	Lois E. Phips	... carcinoma.
	16	Charles J. ...	48	10	26		M	W		...s M. Quimby	Mary Eccleston	... of intest...
Dec.	1	Rolna Stone Shaw				...gold...	F	W	Wife	George ...	Lydia Booth	Heart failure.
	7	...ily F. B...lett	60	10	22		F	M	Housework	...cs	Sally Maria Morse	...
	17	William Oakes	71	8	26	...hf...	M	W	Farmer	Francis Oakes	Mary Ann Mann	Fracture of skull.

DEATHS REGISTERED AT THE COUNTY FARM IN THE TOWN OF HAVERHILL FOR THE YEAR ENDING DEC. 31, 1913.

Month	Day	Name	Yr	Mo	Da	Place of Birth	Sex	Cond.	Occupation	Father	Mother	Cause of Death
Jan.	29	Richard White	60		5		M	M	Pauper			Acute ...
Mar.	4	Harlan Mitchell	66	3	25		M	S	Carpenter			Cerebral ...
	27	Mary Ellis	48			Barnstead	F	S	Pauper			...
Apr.	5	Mary Batchelder	88	9		...elmd	F	W				Old age.
May	20	John Kelley	89	5	8	Lisbon	M	S	Pauper			Senile debility.
July	30	...rd C. Dake	71	1	26	Me.	M	W	Laborer			...oxy.
Aug.	4	Julie Norton	89	2	18	Canada	F	W	Housework			Senile debility.
Sept.	12	Betsy Bacon	86	7	13	Lyman	F	W	"			Old age.
Oct.	7	...e ...h	73			Me.	M	W				Senile gangrene.
Nov.	29	...					F	W				Senile ...
Dec.	1	Ellen Ingerson	56	1	28		F	W	Housework			Arthritis deformans.

I hereby certify that the ...ove return is correct, ...ording to the best of my knowledge ...d belief.

A. F. KIMBALL, ...own Clerk.

CPSIA information can be obtained
at www.ICGtesting.com
Printed in the USA
LVHW021600261118
598291LV00013B/1424